CW00404781

SUNDERLAND
IN OLD PHOTOGRAPHS

ROCK POOL EXPLORATION on the beach in around 1900. The background is very hazy but this is probably Hendon beach.

SUNDERLAND
IN OLD PHOTOGRAPHS

COLLECTED BY
STUART MILLER AND BILLY BELL BEM

ALAN SUTTON

Alan Sutton Publishing Limited
Phoenix Mill · Far Thrupp · Stroud · Gloucestershire

First Published 1991

Copyright © 1991 Stuart Miller and Billy Bell

All rights reserved. No part of this publication may be reproduced, stored in a
retrieval system, or transmitted, in any form or by any means, electronic,
mechanical, photocopying, recording or otherwise, without the prior
permission of the publishers and copyright holders.

British Library Cataloguing in Publication Data

Sunderland in old photographs.
I. Miller, S.T. (Stuart Miller), *1944–*
II. Bell, Billy
942.871

ISBN 0–86299–898–0

Typeset in 9/10 Korinna.
Typesetting and origination by
Alan Sutton Publishing Limited.
Printed in Great Britain by
The Bath Press, Avon.

CONTENTS

SAILING SHIPS on the Wear in around 1910.

INTRODUCTION

THE DEVELOPMENT OF SUNDERLAND

There is evidence of the existence of settlements on the high land around the lower stretches of the River Wear as far back as 9,000 years ago. However, it was not until the arrival of the Angles and Saxons, those avid clearers of woodland, that more permanent settlements were established. It was with the development of a monastic community around the church of St Peter that Wearmouth made its first mark on history as a centre of faith, learning and culture during the great Golden Age of Northumbria. Yet, glorious though this period was, it was, in a sense, a false start. Viking and Scots raiders reduced it to a few splendid remains, a memory and ashes. Despite the efforts of the Bishops of Durham the small borough of Wearmouth was described in 1565 as 'in great decay of building and inhabitants.'

The true history of the town of Sunderland starts in the late sixteenth century with the production of salt from brine which provided a stimulus to the development of a coal export trade. On the basis of ample supplies of coal, other industries rapidly emerged, including the production of lime, alum, copperas and glass. The reluctant royalism of that old opponent Newcastle, and a brief monopoly of the coal trade to London during the Civil War, considerably stimulated the prosperity of the port of Sunderland and the adjacent village of Bishopwearmouth. The key to this prosperity was not coal mining (the Wearmouth Colliery did not produce its first shipment until 1835) but the coal export trade, coordinated by wealthy fitters who brought together the specialisms of the keelmen, casters, trimmers and ballast men, and arranged colliers (not in fact a type of ship, but usually a two-masted brig). One of the greatest obstacles to this trade had been the state of the river but with the establishment of the River Wear Commissioners in 1717 there started the long process of adapting the harbour to the needs of the business community. So successful was the RWC that by the 1830s the problem was one of too much traffic on the river, and so the next three decades were concerned with the creation of dock facilities.

The river was also a considerable obstacle to land communication. Not until 1796 was the famous iron bridge completed, renowned not only for its technology but even more for the controversy over the identity of the designer. Economic growth and the changing pattern of communications affected the spatial development of the community. The combined population of Bishopwearmouth, Monkwearmouth and Sunderland was only 5,000 in the late seventeenth century but by 1801 it was 24,000. The first half of the nineteenth century saw a tendency for better-off people to move away from their fine town houses in the commercial part of Sunderland to live in the more fashionable Bishopwearmouth, a process described by one observer: 'As soon as a man ... feels that he can live at ease he retires to the parish of Bishopwearmouth which comprises the elevated part of the town, wide clean streets and grand houses – in short the West End.'

With the building of the bridge the axis of the town tended to swing away from the High Street and Low Street line to that along Fawcett Street and North Bridge Street. The bridge, the docks and the sinking of the Wearmouth Colliery also stimulated the growth of the rather decayed Monkwearmouth. By the middle of the century the middle class flow was continuing into Hendon and Grangetown, a movement reflected in the survival of much fine terraced housing.

The corollary of this was the decay of the older overcrowded working class areas in the East End, moving Dr François Magendie to protest in 1831 at 'a picture of wretchedness, filth and poverty which ... I could not have believed to exist in the present age in any part of civilised Europe.' It was here that the first outbreak of cholera in the UK occurred in 1831. Despite improvements in sanitation and the redevelopment of the East End from 1851 by the new municipal corporation established in 1837, by the end of the nineteenth century Sunderland still had the highest infant mortality rates in the country and unimaginable depths of squalor persisted.

By this time the wealth of the town was associated more with shipbuilding, and especially with large numbers of small, cheap coastal vessels. As the technology changed from wood and sail to iron and steam the yards of Sunderland adapted accordingly. By the early twentieth century 20,000 men, or about two-fifths of the male labour force, were employed in the industry, and the wealthy shipbuilders were the patrons of art and architecture. However, dependence on the staple industries of coal exporting and shipbuilding left Sunderland very vulnerable in the inter-war depression years.

These years saw the soup kitchens and dole queues as well as the start of the building of extensive council estates and attempts to diversify the local economy by introducing new light industries on trading estates. Full employment returned only with the outbreak of war, but the corollary of this was that wartime conditions maintained a level of protection for relatively inefficient and high cost firms so that when peace returned so did most of the old problems. The post-1945 period has been one of a long, and often painful adjustment during which much of the old community has disappeared but the benefits have not always been obvious.

CHILDREN WITH A ROPE on Hendon beach in around 1900. It is not clear what is at the end of the rope but it is helping to keep Hendon streets quiet.

PHOTOGRAPHS AS HISTORICAL EVIDENCE

There is no doubt as to the value of photographs in revealing aspects of life and labour in graphic form in a way which cannot be matched by documentary archives, however detailed. From the 1880s the combination of the dry-plate process, cheap, small and portable cameras of the early Kodak type and exposure times of less than a second meant that the 'snapshot' amateur photographer was as able as the professional to record people, events and street scenes for posterity. However, while it is true that 'the camera cannot lie' this does not mean that photographs should always be accepted at face value as a truthful record.

The most obvious flaw is the frequent absence of supporting documentary information. The average amateur photographer does not methodically record life for posterity but shoots off 'snaps' of family, friends and scenes and frequently writes no supporting caption. Relatively few people take photographs on behalf of future historians, and since amateur photographers are usually very familiar with their subjects they feel no need to scribble down a description.

Apart from the fact that the interpreter of photographs may have no documentary evidence at all as to who took a photograph, why it was taken and what is shown, there are other problems arising from the selection of subjects which are caused by technological factors and by human propensities.

The main technical problems were the sheer bulk of photographic equipment, the length of exposure times and lighting. The length of exposure times, certainly in the earlier days of photography, eliminated any possibility of spontaneity. This explains why the photographic world of the 1840s appears to be populated by individuals with their heads resting on their hands. By the end of the century, although the process was considerably simplified it was still prolonged and obvious enough to allow people to fix their poses and become totally self conscious. Even though suitable internal lighting apparatus was available by the 1880s it was cumbersome and not for the amateur. The result is that there are relatively few interior photographs. The photographs of children in classrooms in this collection (see section seven) are exceptionally good examples of the relatively few classroom interiors.

As far as human manipulation is concerned, the most extreme type is deliberate falsification. The most often quoted examples are those of Stalinist Russia, where historic photographs were deliberately amended to eliminate disgraced persons. Of course, that is a long way from Sunderland; but William Waples, some of whose photographs are included in this collection, did splice in better quality sky when nature had not been adequately forthcoming. Nor are there any obvious examples of the use of canvas backdrops or the deliberate dressing-up of subjects, in the way which led Dr Barnado to become involved in a famous nineteenth-century court case. However, one must mention in this context the deliberate marshalling of schoolchildren in class photographs so as to hide the shabby and shoeless at the back, or dressing them up from the contents of a 'slop chest'.

It is in the actual selection of subjects that the photographer can, often quite innocently, convey impressions which lead to misinterpretation and create illusions. The ordinary amateur photographer, with the cost of film in mind and an urge to record the memorable, will usually spurn the mundane and commonplace in favour of unusual incidents and people, happy family occasions and picturesque scenery. This selectivity can be misleading for the historian.

For instance, the very high proportion of seaside photographs easily creates an impression that the late Victorian and Edwardian years were a sort of prolonged summer holiday, a Golden Age. There are very many photographs of seaside scenes at Sunderland taken by both amateurs and professionals. The Auty-Hastings Collection is especially noteworthy for some splendid items. In fact they were taken to be converted into postcards for general sale. Similarly, there are large numbers of photographs of carnival days in the East End and Hendon. Not every day of the week was spent at the seaside or in street carnivals however!

Freak and exceptional events encourage a similar distortion. Given the number of photographs of capsized tramcars, travelling by public transport in Sunderland was a hazardous experience. In fact most of them seem to be of the tram which overturned outside the Mountain Daisy public house (see p. 49). There was just one incident but several people visited the area with cameras, especially as it takes some time to raise fallen tramcars. The large number of photographs of celebration days which survive, such as the coronation and silver jubilee of King George V, significant though these occasions were, do suggest that Sunderland was constantly garlanded in flags and bunting.

There are none of the photographs of gypsies with dancing bears, snake catchers, labourers in broderie anglais smocks, or oxen which give an impression, in other areas, that they were typical when, in fact, the reverse was the case. On the other hand, the Grangetown wooden windmill attracted a lot more attention (see p. 88) than the huge brick mill buildings off Green Terrace (see p. 24) which were less photogenic but which actually supplied most of the town's flour.

There is, moreover, an opposite tendency not to take photographs of unhappy occasions. Funerals do not have the magnetic pull of fallen tramcars, although this collection does include one such photograph (see p. 49). Nor do the mundane aspects of everyday life produce many photographs. It is surprising that any pictures of the very typi al back lanes of Sunderland survive, and unusual that they were taken at all (see pp. 58 and 84). Even then one must be cautious. William Waples, for instance, took many photographs in the 1920s and 1930s of the crowded dwellings, courts and alleys of the old East End of Sunderland, and these emphasize decay and squalor. On the other hand, many of these look so squalid simply because they were in the process of being cleared and demolished. Waples was photographing them before they disappeared. Neither Waples nor the largely male photographers of the late nineteenth century would deign to waste film on such everyday scenes as a woman doing her washing, although one such photograph is included (see p. 152).

This lack of consideration for future historians still persists, of course. Most family photographers continue to practise their craft in the same unhelpful way. The future will be well endowed with photographs of children's birthday parties, and of outings to the countryside, theme parks and leisure centres. At the same time, given the pace of change in urban landscapes, parts of the Wearside of only five or ten years ago will be so successfully obliterated by the planners and invincible tarmac layers they will have gone before there was even any thought of recording them for posterity.

Bishopwearmouth

This section is devoted to a visual perambulation around the parish of Bishopwearmouth starting from the parish church. The route followed is down High Street West to the junction with Fawcett Street then along Crowtree Road to Vine Place, down Holmeside and along Fawcett Street and Bridge Street. At several points there are short digressions into some of the side streets. The section concludes with an excursion into some outskirts.

ST MICHAEL'S CHURCH viewed from the west, probably from a window of what would then be St Mary's School, given the angle. The buildings in the foreground (which included the Mayfair toffee factory) were cleared away long ago. This photograph was certainly taken before 1935 because the architect W.D. Caroe added an entrance vestibule as well as surrounding the nave with double aisles between 1932 and 1935, work financed by the shipbuilder Sir John Priestman.

BISHOPWEARMOUTH GREEN lay at the heart of the medieval village. Durham Road, Chester Road, Hylton Road, Stockton Road and High Street West all converge upon what was the village centre. The Green has always been common land. A small railed remnant of it still survives. (Probably Waples)

THE METHODIST COLLEGE ON OLD CHESTER ROAD was originally the Infirmary designed by Ignatius Bonomi and opened in 1823 with sixty beds and an operating theatre, having cost £3,000 to build. In later years it was a training college for Primitive Methodist ministers and a Roman Catholic school. It is now leased by Sunderland Polytechnic. However, its greatest moment was in the winter of 1831/2 when it was at the centre of the struggle against the cholera outbreak. (Flintoff)

LOW ROW seen from the south, probably in the 1920s. The ground falls some twenty feet from the west end of St Michael's church to Low Row. The Burn, or Rector's Gill, used to flow alongside the Row. It is now hidden in a culvert, but it is the same stream which can be seen in Burn Park not far away on the Durham Road.

THE LONDONDERRY. There has long been a public house on this site. In the 1780s it was the Peacock Inn, the chief inn of Bishopwearmouth, a renowned hostelry and coaching inn. In 1831 it was renamed the Londonderry Arms in honour of the third Marquess of Londonderry's newly built harbour at Seaham which opened that year. The present building is more recent. This is an inter-war photograph.

THE CORONATION PARADE of 1911 included representative contingents from a variety of organizations including the police, fire brigade and rocket brigade. The Londonderry is in the background. The bull's head in the top right corner is the sign for the Black Bull public house.

HAYDOCKS SWEET SHOP stood on High Street West opposite the Londonderry. The angle in High Street West at this point probably dates back to the Norman period when such angled entrances to village greens were a common security precaution.

THE PALACE THEATRE was opened in August 1891 by Mr Horace Livermore of Messrs Livermore Bros as a Theatre of Varieties. In its day it attracted some of the greatest theatrical personalities including Vesta Tilley. This photograph was probably taken in the late 1940s when it was a cinema. It was finally demolished in 1973.

THE AVENUE THEATRE in 1932 just before its closure. It stood in Gill Bridge Avenue. When it was opened in 1882 it was the largest theatre in Sunderland and could accommodate 2,500 people. 'Wee Geordie' Wood made his first stage appearance at the Avenue. It was closed in 1932 but its outline has been incorporated into Vaux's Brewery, part of which can be seen just to the right. (*Echo*)

THE HIGH STREET BATHS have been demolished very recently but the façade has been preserved. The building dated back to 1858 when it was opened as a wash-house as part of a programme of public health reform. The entrance to Gill Bridge Avenue is to the right. (Waples)

THE COBDEN EXCHANGE was designed and built by Frank Caws, a great advocate of terracotta façades and concrete flooring. It was claimed this building was indestructible and in 1904 it was put to the test, with some success. It was rebuilt and continued to be used by J.A. Kennedy as a department store. It stood at the top of High Street West. On the back of the postcard from which this is taken a Mrs Matthews wrote to her husband, 'Having beautiful weather here hoping you have the same how do you like this with love wife Bett' (sic).

THE COBDEN EXCHANGE BUILDING in around 1890. Before the building was occupied by Kennedy it was used by Thomas Beardall who specialised in 'pretty bonnets'. This seems to have been a favourite spot for newspaper sellers because there is also a boy standing there in the more general photograph of High Street West shown on p. 22.

VAUX DRAYS IN GILL BRIDGE AVENUE. The Vaux family became involved in brewing in 1805 and set up their first brewery in 1837. It was relocated to premises in Castle Street and Gill Bridge Avenue in 1875 and has remained in the latter, much expanded, ever since. Vaux were one of the first brewers to produce bottled ales and stouts. The Garrison Field is in the background.

THE LIVINGSTONE ROAD DRILL HALL GROUND. The 7th Durham Light Infantry (Sunderland) was based here. The site is now occupied by the police station. The so-called Garrison Field was visited by a fair at Easter and Christmas each year. The 'shuggy boats' can be seen in the background.

High St Sunderland

HIGH STREET WEST between 1900 and 1914. Blackett's was a famous department store which stood at the junction of Union Street and High Street. Lockhart's owned a number of restaurants in the town. Scenes in Sunderland can be dated to some extent by the presence or otherwise of the rails and electricity cables associated with the tramways system. When the Sunderland Tramways Company failed to renew its lease of the corporation lines in 1895 the council decided to purchase and electrify the tramways with the result that overhead cables are visible only after 1900.

HIGH STREET WEST in around 1910. This view is taken from near Kennedy's Grand Clothing Hall in the Cobden Exchange building. There are sale notices in many of the shop windows. Opposite Kennedy's is Crowther and Co., specializing in artificial teeth and advertising the fact rather extravagantly. A number of other shop names and advertisements can also be made out. The boy in the left corner seems to be selling newspapers. There is at least one tram in the background.

CROWTREE ROAD in the 1950s. The name of the street derives, apparently, from the crows and trees which were present in large numbers in earlier days when this section of the town was a pleasant rural area between Bishopwearmouth and Sunderland.

THE KINGS THEATRE in Crowtree Road in 1906 during a performance of *Little Red Riding Hood*. In 1913 it provided a first presentation of moving pictures in the town and in 1915 the first Kinemacolour film. It was taken over by the Blacks brothers in 1918. It was very badly damaged by fire bombs in 1943 and stood derelict until it was demolished in 1954.

WALWORTH WAY linked Crowtree Road and Union Street. With the building of the central bus station and the Bridges shopping centre it has disappeared completely.

ROBSON'S FLOUR MILL stood just off Old Chester Road and behind Green Terrace. The area is now covered by the ring road. The foundations of this mill were revealed again recently while the back lane of Green Terrace was being upgraded.

THE MARITIME ALMSHOUSES. There were several almshouses in the town and these stood between Crowtree Road and Maritime Place. As the name suggests, they were intended for the care of the widows and unmarried daughters of master mariners. Sunderland, of course, had a particular problem in this respect because of the high proportion of seamen in its population. By the middle of the nineteenth century relief had to be provided for an average of 300 widows and 800 children. These almshouses were built c. 1820 but have long since gone.

HOLMESIDE between 1900 and 1914. The north side of the street is still very much the same in general appearance. J. Piper's grocers shop was one of the several shops always remembered for the smell of coffee beans, barrels of butter and blue-bagged sugar.

25

THE OLYMPIA EXHIBITION HALL in Holmeside. The Olympia was opened in 1897 but taken over in 1899 by the Richardson brothers of Kelloe who converted it into a giant Pleasuredrome with roundabouts, gondolas, a circus and a skating rink. Understandably it became the most popular place of entertainment on Wearside. Among other artistes presented 'at enormous expense' were the famous Fossett Family with their legendary circus. Although 'moving picture' shows were introduced on the Olympiagraph it was the competition from cinemas which ended the rule of the Olympia. It closed in 1910. In 1932 Black's Regal was opened on the site, and in 1959 the Regal became the Odeon, part of the Rank chain. The Odeon closed in 1982. It is not clear what is happening in this photograph, perhaps the special performance of Edison George's Special War Pictures of the Boer War in December 1899. (Waples)

THE WHITEHALL RINK in Holmeside in 1908. It is not clear what is happening. The museum, and possibly the newly extended Victoria Hall, can be seen in the distance. Placards reading 'Japan' and 'South Africa' can be deciphered and the Union flag is visible. Policemen are present but it seems to be a fairly amicable occasion. Duckworth's is still a very prominent business in the town although it is no longer in Holmeside. (Waples)

HOLMESIDE seen from the east end in September 1948. It appears that a train has just passed under the bridge. On the corner of Waterloo Place is Maynard's Sweet Shop and a sign advertising Josephs Toy Shop as the local agents for Hornby Trains. The day of the motor car has clearly arrived however. The signs of Turvey's Garage and Binns Motor Stores are very prominent. The former, a long established family firm, was later taken over by Dutton-Forshaw. There is a range of vehicles in the street, and not a one way system in sight! What appears to be a gigantic pair of spectacles is on the roof of the building opposite Maynard's.

A GENERAL VIEW ACROSS MOWBRAY PARK between 1906 and 1914. From the 1840s it was recognized that open spaces for recreational purposes were necessary for the swarming residents of the crowded and rapidly expanding town. The town's building stone was largely quarried from Building Hill and in 1854, when it came onto the market, the council bought it from the Mowbray family for £2,000 and had it laid out as a park by the gardener of the Marquess of Londonderry. In the 1860s an extension to Borough Road was added. It was within part of that extension that the Museum and Art Gallery was built in 1877–79. The Victoria Hall is to the right of the photograph. It was extended in 1906 to the scale shown here. In view of its history there will have been very many people who would have preferred that it be demolished. (Auty-Hastings)

THE WINTER GARDEN was at the rear of the Museum and Library building. It was a conservatory with tropical plants and flowers, an aviary and a pond full of goldfish. It was very badly damaged in 1941 as a result of enemy bombing. This photograph, one of very many of the Winter Garden, was probably taken around 1900. (Auty-Hastings)

THE MUSEUM AND LIBRARY in 1935. Some of the public buildings were specially illuminated as part of the celebrations of the silver jubilee of King George V.

THE VICTORIA HALL stood on Toward Road. It was designed by J. Hoskins of Darlington and built in 1870–72. It was extended by J. Eltringham in 1906 and then destroyed by a German parachute mine in 1941. It was the scene, in June 1883, of a catastrophe comparable only to the Aberfan tragedy. It was built as a hall to be hired out for public meetings and entertainments. On 16 June the event was a show provided by the travelling entertainer Alexander Fay. There was an audience of about 2,000 children, of whom about 1,100 were in the gallery. At the end of the show large numbers of children flooding down the winding staircase, were confronted by an inward closing door which was jammed by the press of bodies and 186 children were crushed and suffocated to death. This photograph was probably taken in the 1920s.

THE OLD EYE INFIRMARY in Stockton Road. The Sunderland and Durham County Eye Infirmary was founded in 1836. These premises were opened in 1893. The Infirmary was financed from donations, legacies, annual subscriptions and a payment of 6d. per patient every three months. There were thirty-six beds and two wards devoted entirely to children.

H.T. HALFPENNY, WINE AND SPIRIT MERCHANT. This shop stood opposite the Eye Infirmary. The photograph is probably pre-1914.

THE MUSEUM AND CENTRAL LIBRARY in around 1910. The building was designed in a French Chateau(-ish) style by J. and T. Tillman. Its foundation stone was laid in 1877 in the presence of ex-President Ulysses S. Grant. This event was preceded by a formal lunch in the Victoria Hall. The design is similar to that of the Bowes Museum at Barnard Castle which had been under construction since 1869. Originally it was intended that a Town Hall should be included but that idea was dropped. The library and a museum gallery were on the ground floor. In 1881 an art gallery was opened on the first floor although the original intention had been to have a school of art and science. In fact, since 1858 there had been a rate-supported public library which was originally housed in the Athenaeum. There was also a subscription library which was established as early as 1795 and which was rehoused in 1878 in a glass-domed lecture hall in Fawcett Street where it remained until it was closed in 1939. On the corner of Borough Road and John Street was the YMCA building which was designed by Frank Caws in 1884. (Auty-Hastings)

BOROUGH ROAD after a heavy fall of snow, probably during the 1880s. There was a great snowstorm in March 1886 and the photograph may have been taken then. Another fall seems to be imminent. Only the strongest-willed photographers venture forth in such conditions!

SAMUEL PINKNEY AND CO. LTD. This shop stood in Norfolk Street. It appears to have been a hardware shop.

FAWCETT STREET in the 1890s. Fawcett Street was laid out between 1814 and the 1840s on land belonging to the Fawcett family. It was part of a whole grid of streets, including John Street, Foyle Street and Frederick Street, laid out by William Jameson. The houses of Fawcett Street were fine three-or four-storey buildings. From the 1870s shops began to spread along the street and this process continued well into the twentieth century. On the left is the polychrome Gothic building which housed the offices of the Gas Company from 1867. It was designed by G.G. Hoskins of Darlington. The classical frontage of the Athenaeum with its fine pillars is visible on the east side of the street. It was built in 1839–41 to house the Literary and Philosophical Society. The Town Hall was built in 1887–90 to a design by Brightwen Binyon. Its clock-tower was a famous landmark. (Auty-Hastings)

FAWCETT STREET in around 1902. There are electric tramcars and the portico of the Athenaeum has been demolished, so this photograph must be after 1900. Vincent's made virtually all of the church organs in the area. The firm still exists but is now based in Durham City. (Waples)

THE CORNER OF FAWCETT STREET in the 1890s. The steps of the Gentlemen's Club can be seen just round the corner from the shop. It was bombed and destroyed in the raid which destroyed Binns in the Second World War.

BINNS STORE in the 1930s. The store had moved from High Street in the 1880s. For some time there were two Binns shops next to each other: one was the store and the other was a cake shop and restaurant. There was no connection. Gradually Binns, the store, expanded and took over.

BINNS STORE following the air raid of 9 and 10 April 1941. The department store on the west side of Fawcett Street was gutted when it was hit by many incendiary bombs. The fire spread from section to section of the building.

THE RETURN OF THE 1937 CUP FINAL TEAM. They have not yet reached this spot. The team arrived at Monkwearmouth station then went on a four mile tour by open coach before parading the cup before 30,000 people at Roker Park. The street decorations were for the coronation of that year. The restaurant is the famous Mengs tea room, one of Frank Caws' terracotta extravagances designed in 1891.

THE WOUNDED SOLDIERS' VICTORY PROCESSION on 19 July 1919. About 18,000 Sunderland men, or ten per cent of the population, joined the armed forces. Of this number, about a third were killed or wounded. A war memorial was erected in Mowbray Park in 1922.

LAYING THE FOUNDATION OF SUNDERLAND TOWN HALL in 1887. As a result of an architectural competition held in 1886 the building was designed by Brightwen Binyon of Ipswich. It was opened in November 1890. It was extended in 1904 because it was too small for its function. In an earlier competition of 1837 a design by Frank Caws was rejected because of a technical infringement of the rules although it was the preferred one.

ON TOP OF A TRAM in Fawcett Street. The date is unknown but judging from the costume it will be the 1890s. Some sort of occasion seems to be being celebrated. It is an unusual subject and angle.

SUNDERLAND CENTRAL STATION in 1938. The station was designed by Thomas Harrison, the company engineer of NER, and built in 1879. The view is towards the ramps at the south end. The main entrance was at the north end, off High Street West. The latter was demolished in 1966 and Littlewoods store was built on the site. (*Echo*)

BOMB DAMAGE TO JOSEPH'S SPORTS SHOP, 6 September 1940. Joseph's Toy Shop is now on Holmeside, but originally the family shop was in Union Street. At 1.13 a.m. on 6 September the central railway station was bombed and a pair of bogey-wheels was thrown through the shop window. A request by Mr 'Monty' Joseph that the LNER remove them was met with the response that it had not put them there! When the LNER did remove the wheels they sent a bill to the firm. (*Echo*)

KING GEORGE VI AND QUEEN ELIZABETH visiting St Thomas' church, one of the victims of the air raid of 14 March 1943. In what was one of the worst air raids on Sunderland seventeen people were killed and thirty-one seriously injured. (*Echo*)

MACKIE'S CORNER in the 1890s. There are no electric tramcar wires and Havelock House is still intact so this photograph must be pre-1898. Havelock House was occupied by the drapery store of George Robinson. Mackie was a silk hat maker and an original tenant of one of the eight shops built as part of Hutchinson's Buildings. These were designed by G.A. Middlemiss in 1850. The corner, like the Gas Office corner, was a famous rendezvous point. There is another Mackie's Corner, with a clock, in Sydney, Australia. It was the very height of athletic achievement to run from Mackie's corner to the Gas Office corner while the Town Hall clock struck twelve.

LOCKHART'S CAFE on 9 July 1898. It stood next to Ward's the tobacconists and opposite Havelock House. The crowd is viewing the damage caused by the Havelock House fire of the previous evening.

THE REMNANTS OF HAVELOCK HOUSE. The fire in this large store broke out on Monday 18 July at about 10.00 p.m. Within a very short period it was an inferno and spread to other shops in the vicinity. The fire brigade, at the time a part of the borough police force, was hampered by the dense crowd. Altogether a total of forty-eight premises were destroyed or very badly damaged. The fire led to the corporation organizing a modern, well equipped fire brigade.

THE HAVELOCK HOUSE in the 1890s. In 1915 the Havelock Cinema was opened on the site of Havelock House and it introduced talking pictures to Sunderland with Al Jolson in *The Singing Fool*. The building next to Havelock House was the Queens Hotel, a 'First-Class Family and Commercial Hotel' opened in 1857. The horse in the right foreground is probably one of the extra horses used to pull wagons up High Street East.

UNION STREET in the 1870s. The view is down towards Holmeside. The central station was later built on the left, but was replaced in turn by the modern Littlewoods store. The famous Blacketts department store later stood on the opposite side of the road.

A GENERAL VIEW OF FAWCETT STREET from the north in the 1890s. Grimshaw's Elephant Tea House was designed by Frank Caws. It was one of the first buildings upon which terracotta was employed. A breathtaking work of extravagant fiction with its elephants and pagodas, Caws intended it as just part of a grand scheme which would convert Fawcett Street to a unique oriental totality! Caws was a very generous man who was much involved with local charities and social work such as the YMCA, Waifs and Strays and Lambton Street Boys' Club.

BRIDGE STREET seen from the south in the 1930s. The Bells Hotel was a famous public house which had a stained glass window depicting Walter Raleigh laying down his cloak for Queen Elizabeth I. Double decker buses only appeared on the streets in the late 1920s. St Mary's Roman Catholic church was built in 1835 to a design by Ignatius Bonomi and reflects the re-emergence of Roman Catholicism from a cautious background. Until 1835 the Sunderland Catholics had worshipped in a small chapel in Dunning Street. On the east side of Bridge Street, near the position of the photographer, was the Grand Hotel, with its 'ground floor ... arranged as a restaurant and buffet tastefully appointed' and its 'sanitary arrangements ... completely in accordance with the latest scientific improvements.'

PANN LANE north from High Street West in around 1877. The Monkwearmouth Junction Railway is under construction and the north tunnel is being built. This involved demolishing, amongst other buildings, the original Grimshaw's Tea House. The NER financed the rebuilding of the demolished properties. The back of St Mary's church can be seen on the right.

THE OLD *ECHO* OFFICE in Bridge Street in around 1954 – at about 12.30 p.m.! The time can be determined because the figure gazing at model trams in the window of Boydell's Toy Shop is Billy Bell himself during his lunch break, caught in a photograph taken without his knowledge, which came into his possession many years later. The famous old *Echo* clock is now at the new *Echo* office. On one side of Boydell's was Johnson's the butchers, and on the other was a supplier of uniforms for merchant navy seamen.

THE SUNDERLAND ROYAL INFIRMARY in around 1900. The Infirmary moved from Chester Road to Durham Road in 1867. The building was designed by Joseph Potts. It was extended several times throughout the 1880s and 1890s. (Auty-Hastings)

CHESTER ROAD in around 1910. (Flintoff)

A FUNERAL IN HYLTON ROAD in the 1930s. The hearses are those of a Mr Cairns who had premises in Hendon and who hired out horses and carriages for all occasions and purposes. The small coffins are those of three children killed in a house fire.

AN OVERTURNED TRAMCAR just outside the Mountain Daisy in Hylton Road on 15 June 1933. (*Echo*)

AN OUTING TO FINCHALE ABBEY in around 1900. These are members of the Sorley Street Congregational church and include the Miss Allen who appears elsewhere in this book hanging out her washing (see p. 152). She is at the top left of the group.

A SORLEY STREET CONGREGATIONAL CHURCH OUTING to Ambleside in around 1910. Miss Allen (later Mrs M. Broadbelt) is seated to the left.

PEMBERTON HALL in 1918. This was a mansion of the Pemberton family, an extensive clan whose wealth derived from a variety of commercial activities but especially from the Wearmouth Colliery. They owned not only this house, which stood on the site of the bowling greens in Barnes Park, but also the hall which is now part of the Ramside Hall Hotel and a hall in Hawthorn Dene.

FEEDING A BIRD IN THE SNOW, in what later became Barnes Park, in around 1910. The woman may have been a servant of the Pemberton family.

THE MONKEY'S LONNIN in around 1900. The lane is now Barnes Park Road. In the background is the vague outline of some houses where Mount Road is today.

RYHOPE ROAD in around 1900. Backhouse Park is over the wall to the right. The old gatehouse still stands.

The East End

Nowadays the old East End is marked by decay and, except in a few patches, by the absence of that strong sense of community which was once its great characteristic. Yet the old river mouth settlement of Sunderland was once a thriving and bustling area where much of the wealth of the town was generated. Since the photographs which follow are, inevitably, largely drawn from the late nineteenth century and twentieth century what is revealed is a predominantly working class district in a state of decline. Many fine buildings survived and still do, albeit in a degraded state, to attest to the former significance of old Sunderland as the heart of the town's economy and the home of wealthy merchant families. Nevertheless, what is very clear from these photographs is a sense of identity which takes generations to create and a couple of decades to destroy.

AN OLD MAN AND HIS DOG somewhere in the East End and probably in the 1930s. Of all the marvellous photographs of Sunderland taken by William Waples in the first thirty years of this century this one is, in its very simple way, probably the most evocative. (Waples)

HIGH STREET EAST in around 1900. What looks like an eagle is, in fact, the phoenix symbol of the famous insurance company. It is still in existence in the yard of a firm in Deptford. The building with the clock was the Seamen's Mission at this time, but in fact it was originally the Exchange Building constructed in 1812–14 to a design by John Stokoe of Newcastle. In 1810 legislation was passed which appointed commissioners to pave, watch and cleanse the streets of Sunderland. They were also authorized to build a market house and this building was the result. One of the distinctive buildings of the town it was, in effect, the town hall. In later years it was structurally altered and used for a variety of purposes. Its future is now uncertain. (Waples)

A GENERAL VIEW OF HIGH STREET in 1851. This is one of the earliest photographs of Sunderland. In the Rawlinson Report of 1851 one witness complained that because the street lights were extinguished too early in the morning the lives of people going to work were endangered by infuriated bullocks escaping from the several slaughterhouses in the side lanes and charging about in the darkness.

THE OLD MARKET in the East End in around 1930. A wide variety of goods and produce were available. It was open for very long hours. On Saturdays it was open from 8.00 a.m. to 12.00 midnight. It was built in 1829–30 as the alternative to the open air market but was not popular with traders because a fee was charged and, from 1832, they were compelled to use it. Its main entrance was in Coronation Street. It was rebuilt in the 1850s and was in use until the mid-twentieth century. (*Echo*)

SMALL BOYS in or near Low Street in around 1910. The activity of the boy in the centre looks very suspicious. At least he has turned his back.

FIGHTING COCK LANE in the 1930s. This sort of lane was typical of the labyrinth of alleys and narrow courts which made up much of the East End.

JAMES WILLIAMS STREET SCHOOL in the 1950s. The street was laid out in the 1870s and was part of an attempt to improve the East End. It was named after one of the prominent reformers. This school was the first purpose built Board School. It was built in 1874 and held up to 1,000 children (all very carefully segregated into 'Boys', 'Girls' and 'Infants').

THOMAS TUGMAN'S GENERAL DEALERS SHOP which stood in Church Street. Next to it was one of the many doss-houses of the East End which had been so condemned by the Rawlinson Report of 1851, one of the stimuli to public health reform in the town.

EAST END ACROBATICS in the 1920s. The photographer set up a few such poses for no obvious reason. (Waples)

A BACKYARD at the back of Long Bank in around 1926. Since backyards rarely warrant a photograph this one is unusual.

E. WEBB'S GENERAL DEALERS SHOP in the 1920s. This stood in Silver Street.

LONG BANK in 1911. The bank joined High Street and Low Street. Just to the right of this scene stood a kipper curing house. The street was demolished to make way for the Corporation Quay which was completed in 1934. Poverty is not necessarily synonymous with squalor; the daughters of even the poorest families were invariably dressed in white starched aprons.

BODLEWELL LANE in 1937. The famous Bodlewell pump is over at the other side of the street. It had once been the sole water supply for most of the households in the area. A 'bodle' was half a farthing and it bought a 'skeel' or two gallons of water. The East End lock-up, which was largely used for the detention of drunks, was very near. Low Street is to the right.

BLUE ANCHOR YARD in the quayside. The old Elizabethan custom house is on the left. This yard was near to the Corporation Quay. The 'Death House' was close by. Bodies found in the Wear, a regular occurrence, were kept there initially.

LOW STREET in around 1910. The carved stone above the sign appears to refer to an 'Entrance' of some sort.

VINE STREET in the 1920s viewed from the north near Prospect Row.

THE VILLIERS HOTEL in Villiers Street in around 1910. John Vipond was the publican. The actual building is still standing. Drysalter and Co. was a small corner shop selling mainly provisions (including the ever present Fry's Chocolate). The scene appears to be that of a day outing about to commence. (Waples)

WEST WEAR STREET, just off East Cross Street. The police station stood in West Wear Street.

HOLY TRINITY CHURCH in Church Street, the parish church of Sunderland. Sunderland was only made a parish in 1719, a very compact parish of 178 acres carved from the much more extensive Bishopwearmouth (which actually ends at Sans Street). The church was one of the very small number built in the North East since the Reformation. The first rector, Daniel Newcome, was described by one source as the 'principal architect', but it is not clear who did actually design this very fine building. The fitting out and decor was the work of William Etty of York, but he was quite capable of designing churches as well and he may have been the architect. Many features of the interior point unmistakably to the church having been the centre of local government as well as a place of worship. The enormous churchyard was taken from the old Town Moor and used until the 1850s. The gravestone of Jack Crawford, the hero of the Battle of Camperdown, is still to be seen there. In the 1840s burials in the graveyard appear to have been rather wet affairs because 'The original strata is composed of strong sound clay. . . . When the graves are excavated down to the clay in some parts of the ground water has . . . to be baled out before the interment can take place.'

AIR RAID PROTECTION TRENCHES being dug in September 1938.

PEOPLE OF TRINITY PLACE near Church Walk in the 1930s. The man with the white waistcoat was Tommy Fox, who worked at North Eastern Marine Engineering and was a ship's fireman. The rest of the group are unknown. The old Sunderland workhouse had been built on the Town Moor in 1740 and was just behind the buildings seen here.

THE AMERICAN BAR in Barrack Street in around 1900.

THE BARRACKS in Barrack Street. The street is still there but the barracks were demolished during the building of the South Dock. They had been opened in 1794 to accommodate about 1,500 men.

A MOTHER AND CHILDREN in Silver Street in around 1900. Nothing is known about this photograph except that the perambulator is said to be home-made (and worthy of a photograph by a proud father!).

MRS GILES AND HER SISTER in around 1890. The photograph of these two old East End ladies was taken by Mr Allen, the father of the Miss Allen shown hanging out her washing on p. 152. He recorded the fact that 'This Lady smoked a pipe', although it is not clear to which one he referred.

THE LONGEST HAIR COMPETITION at the 1912 East End Charity Carnival. Several very excited mothers are standing near by.

THE EAST END CARNIVAL PROCESSION in 1928. The only person known on this float is a Tommy Hopper (just behind the man in the centre). Life-saving equipment is shown and presumably these men were all members of the lifeboat crew or assisted in some way. This scene is at the corner of the Town Moor which, although considerably diminished, was much more extensive in those days. The vehicle is a Sentinel steam wagon.

THE EAST END RAGTIME BAND in 1913. This was one of the regular features of the East End Carnival.

THE FISHWIVES at the East End Carnival in the 1930s. The procession followed a route around the streets of the East End then up High Street East, back down Borough Road, and back to end at the Town Moor.

THE EAST END 'DHOBI WALLAHS' in 1926. They were a cross between a jazz band and a mock drill squad. The photograph was taken in the yard of St John's School.

A STREET PARTY to celebrate the silver jubilee of King George V in 1935. This scene is near to Harrison's Buildings in the East End. The first real council houses, they were opened in 1903 and named after Alderman Harrison. The housewives present will probably include some who, in 1932, brandished frying pans and pelted sausages and black puddings at Miss Agnes Jennings, property manager of the Sunderland Housing Association, who had claimed that 'Poorer women in the town are totally ignorant of household management and any cooking beyond the frying pan.'

ST JOHN'S CHURCH FOOTBALL TEAM in the 1920s. St John's church, a daughter church of Holy Trinity, was built in 1769, financed largely by the wealthy coal fitter John Thornhill. It was closed in 1970 and demolished soon afterwards.

Hendon and Grangetown

As Sunderland grew in the nineteenth century it absorbed the small villages of Hendon and Grangetown. This had been a pleasant rural area with the delightfully named Valley of Love and the spa water of the spring on Hendon beach. In the later nineteenth century it became heavily built up. However, the village sense of community persisted well into this century.

A TRAMCAR TO VILLETTE ROAD. The Hendon-Grangetown district was electrified after 1900. Before then there were horse trams in Tatham Street. The bridge in the photograph carried the railway line between the South Dock and the Penshaw railway. When double decker trams started to operate on this line in the 1930s the bridge had to be raised and the road had to be lowered.

ST PAUL, HENDON. The parish church of Hendon was built in 1852 and could accommodate up to 1,000 people. It was demolished in the 1950s. The colours of the 7th Durham Light Infantry (Sunderland) were laid up here.

ST BARNABAS, HENDON in the 1930s. St Barnabas was built in 1868 at a cost of £4,300. It was bombed in the Second World War and closed from 1941 until the end of the war. It was finally closed in the 1960s.

ANNIVERSARY CELEBRATIONS of the Herrington Street Methodist chapel in 1926. Alderman Cairns (with the large moustache) is in the centre. He was a butcher with a shop in Tatham Street, an elder of the chapel and had been mayor of Sunderland. The occasion would have been one made up of hymns and recitations. The Sunday school is at the front and the Sisterhood at the back. The church was demolished in the 1950s when the congregation moved to Park Road Methodist church.

NORMAN STREET CHAPEL was an outlier of St George's Presbyterian church on Stockton Road. Services were conducted by St George's ministers and local preachers. It was built in the 1880s and demolished in the 1950s.

A SUNDERLAND EQUITABLE SHOP in Emma Street. The 'Pelaw Liquid Metal Polish' advert was a common piece of street furniture. The long shorts are probably those of elder brothers or bought to 'grow into.' The cottages are typical Sunderland cottages, a housing type restricted to this area and the result, probably, of the influence of the Durham pit row and the availability of ample supplies of cheap timber.

THE SHOP OF BILLY PRICE on the corner of Burlington Road and Whitehouse Crescent. His daughter Beatrice is in his arms. The photograph probably dates from the 1930s. Price was a fitter and marker-off at North Eastern Marine Engineering. The shop was a general dealers; it even took in parcels for the Grange Laundry. Dainty Dinah toffee, 'The Sweetest Thing on Earth', was made locally.

ROSS'S FISH SHOP on Nobles Bank Road in the 1920s. Mr Ross and his wife are the two figures to the right.

THE CO-OP SHOP IN HENDON ROAD. Billy Bell's mother worked here when she was sixteen. The Co-op was a vital element in the local economy. Women would allow the 'divi' to build up until the discount, usually nine pence or a shilling in the pound, allowed a worthwhile cash bonus at the end of the month. The photograph probably dates from the 1930s. At one point the future Chief Constable Cook worked there as a boy.

J.T. BUCKNALL AND SON in Hendon Road in the 1930s. Bucknall was a well known local personality who owned a pork butchers shop. A German, his origins led the local populace to smash his windows during the First World War. His saveloys and twopenny 'pork dips' were very popular. The shop was open until 11.00 p.m. on Saturday as were most of the shops on Hendon Road. During the week they closed at about 8.00 p.m.

J. FISHER'S HAIRCUTTING AND SHAVING SALOON on Nobles Bank Road in the 1930s. Fisher was assisted by apprentices starting at the age of 16 years and working there until they were 21. Many men will remember boyhood visits to the 'barbers' lasting hours because their elders and betters were always served first.

J. GRAHAM'S SHOP in Salem Street in around 1910. Graham was a plumber, gasfitter and bellhanger. The adverts include 'Welsbach Incandescent Gaslights' and paints, enamels and varnishes for spring cleaning. The shop was later converted to a fish shop and is now a private house.

BAKER'S BUTCHERS SHOP at Christmas 1921. A vegetarian's nightmare! Mr Baker has a bowler hat on. For normal everyday household cooking his 'parcels', or mixtures of varieties and cuts of meat for half-a-crown, were very popular.

DR CUNNINGHAM about to get into his cab. This scene is in Ward Terrace. The Linden Arms stood in Linden Terrace. The picture is probably pre-1914. The doctor was a well known personality who, together with a Dr Shelley of Ward Terrace, looked after the health of the Hendon residents. He also delivered a lot of local babies.

THE LONDON AND NEWCASTLE TEA COMPANY STORE in Hendon Road in around 1910. The company had another shop in Roker Avenue. It supplied butter and ham as well as tea. 'Pure Indian Tea' was two shillings a pound, but 'Our Famous Tea' was clearly even better.

THE START OF AN OUTING by the Mainsforth Terrace Methodists. The period is probably between 1900 and 1914. Such excursions were usually directed towards Durham, Finchale Abbey or Cox Green.

CAIRNS' STABLES. Mr Cairns rented out funeral cabs and cabs for general use. The stables were in Salem Street. Mr Cairns is to the right on foot and his wife is in the centre of the picture. Judging from the costume this will be before 1914.

CHILDREN ON HENDON BEACH in around 1900. This photograph is typical of the vast number of seaside photographs available for Sunderland. The docks are in the background. The beach was very popular with local residents. The stream running through Backhouse Park went into culverts in the Valley of Love (or the 'cundies' as they were known locally) then came out at the beach.

THE VILLIERS ELECTRIC THEATRE was Sunderland's first purpose-built cinema. It held up to 1,000 patrons. It stood in Villiers Street and opened in January 1912 with *The Great Mine Disaster*. It was run in conjunction with the Roker Cinema. It closed on 16 March 1958 with the Disney film *Rob Roy*. The synagogue was next to it. The Hudson Road School was on the other side of the street and was known as the 'jews' school' because so many jewish children attended it. (*Echo*)

THE LORD ROBERTS stood on the corner of Winchester Terrace and Mabel Terrace. It was built in 1900 at the height of the popularity of Lord Roberts, the Commander-in-Chief in South Africa. There used to be a painting of 'Bobs' in the window. This photograph was probably taken in the 1950s, not long before it was demolished.

THE DIVAN was also known as the Little House. It was owned by Tommy Little who was well known as an organizer of trips to the away fixtures of Sunderland AFC in the 1930s. He also owned an off licence in Hendon Valley Road (and there is still one on the same site). The curiously named public house stood on Hendon Road. It was demolished in the 1950s.

THE ODDFELLOWS ARMS on the corner of Robinson Terrace. The owner, a Mr Stratton, owned several public houses and started a coach business which developed into Redby Coaches Ltd. His son Fred Stratton, the owner of the coach firm, died in 1990. To the right of the Oddfellows was Wood's butchers shop which stood on the corner of Norman Street.

THE INTERNATIONAL HOTEL in International Road. The well known 'Nash' stood on the corner of International Road and Ethel Street. Before it became a public house it was part of the house of the Bramwell family, one of the wealthy families of Hendon (and the source of several of its street names such as Bramwell Road, Henry Street and Mabel Terrace).

HENDON RAGTIME BAND in Winchester Terrace in the 1920s. They were a regular feature of the Hendon Carnival which used to be held in Hendon Burn and involved a parade around the streets. The money raised went to charity. The carnivals were organized by street committees and were quite formal affairs. Harlequins, 'toffs', red indians and a couple of 'women' are in this group.

THE HENDON ALLOTMENTS ASSOCIATION playing bowls at their grand opening at Corporation Road. A Mr Meek is sixth from the right.

TEACHERS AT HENDON BOARD SCHOOL in 1885. It was a group of teachers at this school who met in October 1879 at the British Day School in Norfolk Street and formed the Sunderland and District Teachers Association Football Club which became the Sunderland Association Football Club. It played at first at the Blue House Field near Hendon School (the first of six grounds). Second from the right at the back is James Allan who, more than anyone, was the founder of the team. Raich Carter, the captain at the FA Cup Final in 1937, was born in Hendon and went to the Board School.

THE BACK LANE OF HENRY STREET or Ford Street. The photograph is claimed to be from the 1920s but it is really ageless and very typical. The hatchways for the dry closets or 'netties' can be seen. These were cleared at night by corporation 'night soil men'. Local children sang a largely unprintable song which started, 'Me father was a midnight mechanic./He worked all day and he worked all night./And when he came home in the morning . . .'. The rest may be left to the imagination.

BOMB DAMAGE AT ETHEL STREET in September 1940. No-one was killed. This was near the junction with International Road. The old warehouse in the background had been a mill. The fortunate Price family had moved out of their house just a week before. Good eyesight will be able to pick out a cat in the centre. (*Echo*)

THE WRECKAGE OF A HEINKEL III shot down on 6 September 1940. It crashed into a house and air raid shelter in Suffolk Street. Of the Stormont family, the mother was killed, the father very badly injured and the teenage daughter Jean lost both of her hands. Unexploded bombs from this plane led to the evacuation of houses around Robinson Street for two months. (*Echo*)

THE WRECKAGE OF VALLEY ROAD SCHOOL in October 1942. On 11 October a number of phosphorous 'firepot' bombs were dropped on Hendon. They did little damage but a 1,000 kilo bomb destroyed twenty houses and one side of Valley Road School. Seven people were killed and twenty-one seriously injured. (*Echo*)

LAYING THE FOUNDATION STONE of the new Valley Road School on 20 October 1948. The stone was laid by Alderman William Harvey, the chairman of the Education Works Sub-Committee. Presumably these girls will have been involved in some singing and recitations at the event.

GRANGETOWN WORKMEN'S CLUB OUTING in the 1920s. Billy Bell's grandfather John is the man with the pipe.

PRYDE'S BAKERY VAN on Ryhope Road at Grangetown before 1914. The bakery was in Hendon and went on to become a very large company. Mrs Greathead is standing in the doorway of her shop.

A GENERAL VIEW OF GRANGETOWN in 1908. The electrified tramcar extensions to Grangetown and Villette Road will not have been long opened.

THE POST WINDMILL AT GRANGETOWN. The mill stood in the area now occupied by the St Aidan's Estate. It ceased operating before 1914. Quite a number of photographs of it exist. It was not demolished until the early 1950s.

Monkwearmouth, Roker, Fulwell and Seaburn

In this section we cross the Wearmouth Bridge and enter the world on the north side of the River Wear. In the past these were distinct villages in their own right and Fulwell certainly still has that air about it. The destination of this journey is, of course, the very attractive seafront.

THE LAST FOOTBALL CROWD to cross the old Wearmouth Bridge in 1928 before work started on its successor. They look as grim and disbelieving as any group of supporters of Sunderland AFC would do today.

THE WEARMOUTH BRIDGE in around 1900, viewed from the Bishopwearmouth end. There are tram rails but no overhead cables. The evidence of horses is fairly clear though.

THE WHEATSHEAF LIGHTHOUSE, around the 1940s. The date is suggested by the Austin 10 motor car, the sodium lights and what appears to be a Morris army lorry. There was a police box on this site from the 1930s. The view is down Roker Avenue. Next to the Lighthouse Stores is the Miners' Hall and the Salvation Army Hostel. Roker Avenue was a product of the Sunderland Extension Improvement Act of 1867 which gave the council power to build housing for working class people to rent or purchase. (*Echo*)

THE WHEATSHEAF in the 1940s. This could be a wartime photograph. Belisha beacons were introduced when Hore-Belisha was Minister of Transport in 1934. To the north of the Lighthouse Stores stood the church of the Venerable Bede, a Church of England church built in 1870. The Wheatsheaf public house, which gave its name to this well known junction, is still there but in the 1930s its neighbour was the depot of Sunderland Tramways. There has been a Wheatsheaf on this site for a long time. The owners of the predecessor of this one enjoyed an indirect income from customers referred to in the Rawlinson Report of 1851 thus: 'Wheatsheaf inn – Here I found a large middenstead full of all kinds of filth, where it was allowed to remain until it was sold to the highest bidder, and then it was allowed to remain to suit their convenience. . . .' The wooden lighthouse stood above a shop which, in its last guise, was a sweetshop and tobacconists. It was a replica of the very famous octagonal lighthouse which stood on the old North Pier until its demolition in 1903.

THE CORA PICTURE PALACE around the 1920s. Next to it stood a blacksmiths and cartwrights business owned by W.H. Sutton. These, and other buildings, stood at the corner of Southwick Road and Newcastle Road. The Cora, which was demolished in 1982, was more properly named the Coronation Picture Palace, for so it was called in 1911. However, the owners gave way to the local fashion very soon. From 1911 until 1948 it was owned by James H. Tindle, then by his wife until it was closed in 1959. Tindle also owned a fleet of charabancs and the father of the actress Christine Norden was employed by him as a driver for some time.

MAYPOLE DAIRY CO. LTD in Southwick Road, beside the Wearmouth Colliery. This was a grocers shop. In fact there were several Maypole shops in the town.

Opening of the Bowling Green, (24th May 1930), Wearmouth Colliery Welfare Ground.

THE OPENING OF THE BOWLING GREEN in the Wearmouth Colliery Welfare Ground in 1930. Presumably the colliery manager is 'laying the jack' at 3.00 p.m. precisely. The young woman with her hand on her hip is determined to miss nothing.

Newcastle Road, Sunderland.

NEWCASTLE ROAD in around 1900. The chapel on the corner of Joannah Street was designed in 1877 by John Eltringham and would have been Welsh Presbyterian when this photograph was taken. It is now the National Spiritualist church.

FULWELL MILL in the early 1950s. The house was occupied by a family called Moodie. It was demolished in the later 1950s. The Fulwell Mill was built in 1821. It is the most complete mill standing between Humberside and the Firth of Forth. It was last used in 1949, although an engine was employed rather than the wind vanes. The sails were replaced in 1986 and the mill was reopened to the public in March 1991 after a lengthy period of restoration. A very vivid landmark, it is made of magnesian limestone.

FULWELL MILL seen from near Fulwell railway station.

FULWELL INFANTS' SCHOOL IN 1911. The children seem to be being marshalled into a coronation procession. The school was built in 1877 and was demolished a century later. At this time there was a farm to the north of it and a blacksmiths to the south.

FERRY'S FARM at Fulwell in around 1910. The farm stood to the north of Fulwell Infants' School. There were several farms in this area at the time. The farm was bombed in the Second World War.

J.W. STORES' SHOP in 1902. This general store stood at the corner of Sea Road and Fulwell Road and opposite the Bluebell public house. The true name of Fulwell's main thoroughfare is Seaview Road, but the name seems to have been abbreviated simply because the nameplate was broken! The Stores family is standing in the doorway.

THE BLUEBELL public house in around 1900. Its modern equivalent is as much a rendezvous point as its predecessor appears to have been.

W. PRATT AND SONS, FRUITERERS. This shop stood in Roker Avenue. This photograph is probably from the period 1900–1914. Mr Pratt is on the left and his wife is on the right. They also owned a seafront kiosk on the lower promenade. As well as fruit, the Pratts seem to have acquired a stock of rabbits.

THE STOCKS on Look-Out Hill, Hallgarth, Monkwearmouth. It was also known as Cage Hill. This was once at the heart of the so-called 'Barbary Coast'. The lock-up was used to accommodate drunks. These gentlemen are merely posing.

PROMENADE ROKER. 1005. *Auty*

THE TERRACE AT ROKER in around 1900. Much of the promenade development took place in the 1860s when it was a means of employing men during a period of recession. In fact the Roker and Seaburn seafront was not developed until after the 1880s, probably because it was too close to the working class district of Monkwearmouth to be attractive to the middle classes. Roker Baths Road did, however, allow easy access to the Roker Baths Hotel. (Auty-Hastings)

ROKER SANDS .1061 .Auty

ROKER SANDS in around 1900. The building of the great breakwaters is dealt with elsewhere (see p. 110). Apart from the crane and the fact that the people of the day were rather more reluctant to undress in public, this is a very familiar scene in a photograph which almost conveys the sound of the waves. Roker and Seaburn were very popular with holiday makers in the earlier years of this century, indeed until beyond the Second World War. Miss Sidd of Consett, who sent a postcard with this scene on it in 1905, certainly enjoyed her stay here because she wrote to her friend, Ada, 'Miss Robinson and I enjoying ourselves a treat. We have champion lodgings it is lovely weather ... It's a treat to having nothing to do.' Mrs Bradwell of Ryhope also chose this card to write to a friend, 'I am much about the same. I feel a little fresher every morning they says I am doing well. Yours truly W.B.' (Auty-Hastings)

AN UPTURNED BOAT used as a shed by fishermen at the North Dock in around 1900.

A DONKEY RIDE on the beach in around 1900. The view is taken on the south side of the Roker breakwater. The ponies and donkeys were owned by a family called Smith who lived in Brandling Street, where they were kept in a large back yard. Presumably neighbours were less sensitive in those days. Little Hubert Vickers, on holiday at Roker in 1908, was obviously a 'regular' for he wrote, 'Another fine day. Just off for another Donkey ride. I am a very good boy.'

ROKER PARK in around 1900. The land originally belonged to the Williamson family and the Ecclesiastical Commissioners, who presented it to the corporation to be laid out as a public park. It was opened in 1880. The drinking fountain was erected in that year.

THE PIERROTS SHOW at the lower promenade entrance to Roker Park before the First World War. There are lots of photographs of the Pierrots which were a very popular attraction.

THE ROKER PARK FOOTBRIDGE during the Illuminations in 1938. The original Illuminations started in 1937, stopped during the Second World War and then were resumed until the 1950s. The road bridge was built over the ravine in 1880 so enabling development to start in the form of fine terraced housing. The famous Spottee's Cave is one of the many caves which honeycombed the cliffs at this point. Spottee was, reputedly, a shipwrecked Frenchman who lived in the cave in the early nineteenth century. He was fortunate to be washed ashore at Sunderland rather than Hartlepool!

ON THE BEACH AT ROKER just before the First World War. The boy on the right seems to have a very large bandage on his head. This was the scene on a postcard used by a Mrs Pratt of Millfield to write to a Mr White. 'Just . . . to tell you I'll be expecting you on Wed. morning to paper and whitewash for me . . .' Some people never relax! (Auty-Hastings)

'JOYLAND - TOYLAND' at Holey Rock in the 1920s. The crevices and caves gave this local landmark its name rather than any religious significance. That it was a source of potential danger can be seen by the fact that the most tempting holes were bricked up and there is a warning about 'falling stone'. Holiday makers could buy hot water, ice cream, one penny drinks, a 'real nice cup o' tea' and other refreshments at the 'Picnicers Headquarters' where there were also tables and shelters. For sixpence ('ladies half price') couples could dance from 8.00 p.m. to 11.00 p.m., or till midnight on Wednesdays and Saturdays, and 'under ideal conditions' as well!

HOLEY ROCK before 1914. There used to be a gun battery on the cliff above and the point was known as Battery Point. The Rock was destroyed after the Second World War because it was a dangerous attraction for small boys.

THE LOWER PROMENADE AND SANDS. Lockhart's had several restaurants in the town.

THE CEREMONIAL OPENING OF THE BEDE CROSS at Roker on 11 October 1906. This very good replica of a Saxon cross commemorates the life and achievements of Wearside's greatest son (who probably lived in Jarrow in fact).

TENTLAND, Seaburn, in the 1920s. Large numbers of bulky canvas tents were stored on the promenade and rented out to sun-seekers for the day.

THE NEW PROMENADE at Seaburn. In 1902, according to the Sunderland Coronation Souvenir, 'Beyond Roker there are now being built the first houses of a new village "Seaburn".' By 1920 the area was still made up largely of open fields. The Seaburn Hotel was yet to be built. The much frequented Alex Hastings shop was also a feature of the future as, of course, was the notorious fountain!

HMS SENTINEL AGROUND AT SEABURN in 1921. This cruiser carried Sir John French and his staff to France in August 1914. It was on its way to the Tyne to be broken up when it drifted ashore on the beach near to the area where the Seaburn Hotel is today.

The Harbour and the River

The role of the River Wear in the history of the development of the town has, as with all rivers and towns, three aspects to it. On the one hand it has been a thoroughfare for the transportation of people and goods. As such it has also been, for some people, a means of earning a living. However, the Wear has also been a considerable obstacle to development and a large part of the story of Sunderland has been the overcoming of difficulties posed by a narrow, meandering and shallow river, only too eager to choke itself with silt.

THE HARBOURMASTER'S LAUNCH in the 1890s. In the background is the RWC dredger and a hopper used to carry the dredged material out to sea. On land in the background is the North Sands shipyards of Joseph L. Thompson and Sons Ltd. At the time of this photograph Thompson's headed the tonnage output on the Wear and had been in fourth position in the world league of production. The captain of the boat is in the bows and the harbourmaster is in the centre. The first steam powered mechanical dredger in the world was used on the Wear in 1797.

THE SEA ENTRANCE TO THE SOUTH DOCK in around 1880. One of the several novel features of the South Dock, built between 1846 and 1856, was its sea entrance in Hendon Bay. In fact it was a failure and had to be fitted with a wider and more conventional lock between 1878 and 1880.

HENDON DOCK UNDER CONSTRUCTION in around 1865. In 1859 the Sunderland Dock Company, which built the South Dock, was taken over by the RWC. Even the large 66 acre dock was, by then, too small and between 1864 and 1868 the Hendon Dock was added.

MOUTH OF THE WEAR .1004. CLS.

THE MOUTH OF THE WEAR in around 1900. The lower stretches of the River Wear were virtually rebuilt by the RWC who, almost from their foundation, were engaged in building piers. The old inner South Pier is the much amended and repeatedly reoriented descendant of that built between 1725 and 1730 and, in its day, one of the wonders of the world of river engineering. The inner North Pier was added between 1785 and 1795. On the latter is the famous octagonal lighthouse built in 1801–2 by the harbour engineer Jonathan Pickernell (the pioneer of steam dredging). It was this lighthouse which had to be winched bodily to the end of the extended pier in 1841, upright and on a wheeled cradle. It was demolished in 1903. On the inner South Pier is the wrought iron lighthouse, produced in 1856 by the harbour engineer Thomas Meik, which now stands above the cliffs at Roker. The Roker breakwater is under construction in the left background. (Auty-Hastings)

THE START OF WORK ON THE ROKER BREAKWATER in 1883. The idea of outer 'covering piers' was a very old one and there was some exploratory work in the late eighteenth century. It was following a report by Sir John Coode in 1876, with some design amendments by the harbour engineer Henry Wake, that work began on the first of these two distinctive features of the harbour. The foundations were a natural rock outcrop supplemented with bags of cement deposited both manually and also by a specially designed boat.

THE FIRST BLOCKS of the Roker breakwater were laid by hydraulic crane on 24 August 1885. Until the last blocks were laid in 1902 the huge 290 ton crane was a very visible feature of the town.

THE FINAL BLOCKS of the Roker breakwater being put into position in 1902.

THE ROKER BREAKWATER still incomplete in 1902. 'Final blocks' (above) is rather a misleading description. The round head of the breakwater was built separately so the gap still remained to be filled. The ceremonial opening took place on 23 September 1903, with the Earl of Durham in attendance, when a polished black commemorative block was placed on the new lighthouse.

THE CHANNEL SQUADRON visiting Sunderland in September 1903. The railway line had been used for the construction of the Roker breakwater. Work had started on the South breakwater in 1893. In 1912 it was decided not to proceed any further and conclude it with a round head. The two great harbour works clearly justified their advocacy by Thomas Meik, who in 1849 remarked that ' . . . by completely breaking up the sea before it enters between the piers (they) will ensure internal tranquility . . . ' (Auty-Hastings)

A CAISSON in the North Dock in 1900. It was used in the construction of the South breakwater, built by Doxfords for the RWC. The North, or Wearmouth Dock was designed by the incomparable Isambard Brunel, although most of the local work was probably done by his assistant Francis Giles.

QUAYSIDE ACTIVITY.

A CARGO VESSEL aground in the harbour in around 1912. The lifeboat is near and there is a line attached to the ship. The South breakwater is in the background. The name appears to be *Arendal*.

A WRECKED SHIP at the south outlet of the South Dock in 1885.

A THREE-MASTED SAILING SHIP being towed by a tugboat. The hawser is just visible. Bartram's shipyard is in the background. This is probably before 1914.

THE FISH QUAY in the South Docks with three paddle tugs alongside. The buildings in the background are grain warehouses, one of which was designed by John Dobson. These landmarks were under sentence of destruction at the time of writing.

THE *IANE*, with the hailing house and the pilot house in the background. This coble was owned by a well known local fisherman called Morse. She acquired her strange name from the initial letters of the Christian names of the children of the owner: Irene, Alan, Norman and Elizabeth. She was used to carry the cables to the Dutch tugs used to refloat the *Birtley* in 1935.

A PILOT COBLE near the south outlet. These sailing cobles would go as far as Flamborough Head to pick up ships. This frequently involved a race for business. They carried four men: two to pilot the ship and two to bring the coble back.

THE SUNDERLAND FERRY landing on the North Sands side of the river. The *Vint* is approaching. The toll was a halfpenny, although people living in houses belonging to the Williamsons, the major landowners on the north side, were given tokens to allow them free passage. This looks as if it is during the 1950s. The shipyard of J.L. Thompson is beyond the wall which was intended to stop shipyard workers escaping from work too early!

A GENERAL VIEW OF SHIPPING ON THE WEAR in the 1920s. Wylams Wharf (known as the Cement Quay) is on the left. Beyond that are the Scotia Engine Works. The ferry boat in mid-river is the *Sir Walter Raine* or the *Vint*. The small boat with the predominantly white funnel is the *Cinema Star*, a tugboat owned by the RWC and used to tow ballast hoppers.

A RIVERSIDE VIEW from near the fish quay in 1930. The vessel with the vertically striped funnel section is one of the Fenwick tugboats. The RWC *Cinema Star* is to its right and a couple of hoppers are to the left.

A GENERAL VIEW OF THE RIVER in the 1950s. The two vessels to the right are of the Silver Line, built by J.L. Thompson's. The Scotia Engine Works can be seen on the south bank. In 1900 it had been amalgamated with other firms in Hartlepool and Middlesbrough to form Richardsons, Westgarth & Co. Ltd. The Scotia Works was well known for good labour relations. It was there that the eight hours movement was inaugurated in 1892.

A SAILING SHIP UNFURLING in around 1910. The vessel in the foreground seems to be preparing to go to sea. The small foyboats carried hawsers to buoys in the river.

THE BRIDGES, viewed from downstream in around 1910. In this superb photograph there is almost the sound of paddle-wheel blades beating the water and the smell of industrial smoke. In mid-stream is the dredger and a hopper. On the south side of the river can be seen the bottleworks at Bishopwearmouth Panns. The railway bridge, designed by Thomas Harrison, was built in 1879 and was the last link in the Monkwearmouth Junction line. The road bridge had been built in 1858–9 on the site of the original Wearmouth Bridge and was designed by Robert Stephenson. The ribs of the old bridge were kept in place although they were no longer easily visible. (Auty-Hastings)

THE BRIDGES, viewed from Austin's shipyard in the 1920s. (Waples)

12·11·28.

THE NEW WEARMOUTH BRIDGE under construction in November 1928. The present bridge was designed by Mott, Hay and Anderson and was built in 1927–9 around the old one so as to keep the traffic moving. Not a fragment of the original Wearmouth Bridge seems to have survived so that the second iron bridge in the world and the most famous landmark of Sunderland has disappeared without a trace. Just visible on the north side of the bridge is the curiously named Bromarsh Cinema, one-time Black's Waxworks Exhibition, converted in 1906 into Sunderland's first permanent cinema. Originally it was called the Monkwear-mouth Picture Hall but after an interlude as the Bridge Cinema it became, in 1919, the Bromarsh, an anagram of the first few letters of Marshall Brothers, its then owners. It was destroyed in May 1943 by enemy bombs.

THE FIRST WEARMOUTH BRIDGE in the mid-1850s. This very early photograph, taken by Edward Backhouse, does justice to a bridge which was described by one of its admirers in 1841 as:

... one of those projections which show the power of man so strikingly, and which well entitle the engineer to exclaim *'nil desperandum'*! – Looks light and woven like the spider's meshes which that insect has spun in the air, across some vast chasm.

(Dr A.B. Cranville, *Spas of England*, 1841)

The second iron bridge in the world is still the subject of some controversy as to who was the designer, with one claimant being the famous republican Thomas Paine. The legal inventor of the design was the Castle Eden banker Rowland Burdon, who patented the system in 1795, but while there is no doubt that he was the chief proponent and financial backer, the real designer was probably Thomas Wilson, a local schoolmaster. In this picture the six arch ribs, their component cast iron blocks and the lateral tubes which held the ribs together can all be seen.

A VIEW DOWNSTREAM FROM THE WEARMOUTH BRIDGE in 1905. The most prominent feature is the timber yard and works of J. and W. Wilson and Sons, timber importers. The decline of shipbuilding with timber was reflected in the fall in imports from 147,900 loads in 1874 to 77,119 loads in 1912. Wilson's were the most significant of the importers.

THE TUNNELS near to the Lambton and Hetton Drops. Tank Engine No. 39 and the Teamer's Shed are on the left. The Lambton tunnel is on the left and the Hetton tunnel on the right. Billy Bell worked at the Lambton Drops in the 1950s. The coal was 'teamed' into the waiting vessels by a 'teamer' who knocked a bar which opened the bottom of wagons and allowed coal to pour down the chutes.

THE WATER BOAT MAN. The *Olive Branch* was owned by Mr Scott who took fresh water to the ships in the river and the docks. He was 93 years of age when he died in the 1980s. In the background are the Hetton Drops.

A DOXFORD'S TURRET SHIP being launched in 1900. Turret ships had very considerable cargo capacities and a deck which was raised along the centre rather than flush. It is claimed that one of the reasons for the design was to reduce the deck area in order to reduce passage charges at the Suez Canal. This ship seems to have got stuck while being launched however. By the time this picture was taken about eighty such steamers had been launched by Doxford's, varying in size from 1,000 to 9,000 tons deadweight.

A DOXFORD'S SAILING SHIP in the 1860s standing in the South Dock. Doxford's started to build steam ships in 1878.

TORPEDO BOAT DESTROYERS alongside Doxford's yard in the 1880s. There is no sign of work on the Queen Alexandra Bridge. The destroyers built by Doxford's at this time were powered by oil-burning steam engines, but from the 1890s they had turbines.

A ROYAL VISIT TO DOXFORD'S on 15 June 1917.

THE *RECLAIMER* in the 1930s. This vessel was used as a salvage ship, but was also hired by Trinity House to supply their lighthouses and refit lifebuoys.

THE SCOTTISH FISHING FLEET in the South Dock in the 1930s. These trawlers used to visit Sunderland every year as they followed the herring shoals.

THE *PRESIDENT* TUGBOAT near the Folly End. The anchor symbol was used by the Fenwick Fleet. There is another tugboat behind her with the same markings.

THE FIRE BOAT *FIRE QUEEN*. She was one of two such craft. The *Fire King* was in the docks and the *Fire Queen* in the river. A Fenwick collier stands behind her. The Fenwick's were a very famous shipping line whose colliers had names which always ended with '-*wood*'.

THE *ZEALOUS* in 1942. She had been damaged during an air raid. The *Fire Queen* is alongside pumping water out of her. There were no casualties. The *Zealous* was a general cargo merchant ship. She is believed to have been one of the vessels used to salvage the submarine HMS *Thetis* which sank in 1939 with the loss of all but three of those on board.

THE *ELLA SAYER* on fire in the South Dock during the First World War. Two fire boats and a tugboat are with her.

THE *TYNEHOME* standing in the South Dock. The *Tynehome* belonged to Common's shipping line. In the First World War she was used as a Q-ship, a disguised and heavily armed decoy ship used to attract U-boats into surfacing to make an easy kill only to be destroyed themselves. The Commons lived in a house in the Cedars which was, at one time, called Tynehome. In 1940 the ship struck a mine and sank.

THE *CORSAIR* TUGBOAT with a collier in tow during the Second World War. The carley survival rafts are quite prominent. The shipyard of J.L. Thompson is on the left side of the photograph.

THE QUEEN ALEXANDRA BRIDGE under construction. The bridge was designed by Charles A. Harrison for the North Eastern Railway and Sunderland Corporation and constructed by Sir William Arrol and Co. Ltd. It was designed to carry coal trains from west Durham to the South Dock. By the time it was opened in 1909 the coal traffic had started to decline and the 'double decker' bridge has always been something of a white elephant.

THE HYLTON FERRIES in the 1890s. Until 1796 they served the main route between Sunderland and Newcastle. The chain-operated ferry was used for vehicles and the rowing boat for passengers. The latter was in use until 1957. The ferry was a favourite subject of the artist Ralph Hedley. In the background is the Golden Lion public house.

Some of the Workers

Many workers have already been seen incidentally in the photographs of locations and events. In this section the emphasis is very much upon people at work, or rather looking into the camera in a self-conscious manner while at work (except for Miss Allen, who is too busy for anything of the sort!).

HENDON COMPANY LIFE SAVING ASSOCIATION in 1910. The photograph was taken at the Rocket House on the cliffs at Grangetown. Billy Bell's grandfather is sitting second left in the second row. He was born in 1860 and died in 1942 having worked in the paper mills until he was 74. In 1914 he gave the wrong age and joined up then went on to fight at Gallipoli, the Somme and Passchendaele. The line up includes representatives of many of the well known Hendon and Grangetown families such as the Toughs, the Naisbys and the Greatheads.

LIFE SAVERS WITH ROCKET APPARATUS at the Rocket House on the South Docks in around 1910. Rockets were used to carry a rope to a ship in distress so that a breeches-buoy could be hauled to the vessel and the crew rescued. The man on the right is holding a hailer.

THE *FLORENCE NIGHTINGALE* in 1865. This was Sunderland's first lifeboat. The coxswain is standing on the stern. At one time there were no less than four lifeboats based at Sunderland: one in the North Dock, one in the South Dock, one at Grangetown and the other at the south entrance of the South Dock.

THE FOREMEN of the Shipyard Department of Doxford and Sons before 1914. These men were the foremen of various departments such as the cutters, platers, caulkers and riveters. The firm was started by William Doxford in 1840 at Pallion. The great growth of the firm came after 1892 when the first Turret steamer was launched. Orders poured in for these vessels which had hulls virtually totally devoted to cargo carrying.

THE GRANGETOWN LIFEBOAT on the beach at Grangetown in 1910. Billy Bell's grandfather is there somewhere but, in the absence of the pipe usually clenched between his teeth, is not identifiable.

DOXFORD'S PLATERS AND HUMPERS just before 1914. The plates were bought in then marked off and punched by the platers. The plates were riveted into place using rivets heated in a bellows-powered coke fire which were thrown up to catcher boys who caught them in a bucket.

LADY HUMPERS WORKING WITH PLATERS at Austin's during the Second World War. There was a view that the employment of women during the First World War had tended to 'positively retard production rather than to help it,' and by October 1942 women constituted only 1.3 per cent of the shipyard labour force.

THREE MEN AND A MACHINE, 15 October 1909. It is not clear what these men are supposed to be doing. Indeed, judging from their expressions they are not too sure either! The general context suggests that they are involved in some sort of timber fabrication.

A BORING-OUT TEAM in 1935. These men were employed in boring-out the stern tube for the propellor shaft. A boring machine stands in the background. Billy Bell's brother, James, is seated to the left. He was decorated for valour in 1941 and later captured by the Japanese. The chargehand fitter in white overalls was their father. The photograph was taken at Burnt Island in Scotland where the team had been sent to work temporarily.

THE MACHINE SHOP of the North Eastern Marine Engineering Company between 1910 and 1914. This is where the castings were machined. In the centre is the table used in the marking off of pipes and castings. The works were on the east side of the South Docks. Together with the works at Wallsend, the establishment was the largest of its type in the world.

ONE OF THE DIVERS of the River Wear Commissioners. This is probably a Mr Scott who lived in a house in the South Docks.

A DEMONSTRATION BY THE FIRE BRIGADE in the station yard in 1908. The brigade had been newly established as a result of the Havelock House fire of 1898 (see p. 43). The fire station on High Street West was designed by W. and T.R. Milburn and opened in 1908.

POLICE FIREMEN outside the West Wear Street police station. These were the men called out to deal with the Havelock House fire of 1898. The station in West Wear Street (off East Cross Street) was the first station built in Sunderland. The original site was purchased in 1842 but the premises were extended several times.

THE FIRST POLICE PATROL VAN. The Traffic Department was established in 1931 and it provided mobile patrols. This vehicle would be what was called a 'Black Maria'. The date on the photograph is 1938 but it looks much earlier. The man on the right looks a very 'likely lad'!

THE SUNDERLAND CORPORATION WATER CAR after modification in 1907. It is not clear what the fault was before modification but the jet of water seems to be a cause of some pride.

AN OPEN DECKED TRAM at the Wheatsheaf tram depot in 1916. The staff are a foreman, a cleaner, a driver and two conductresses. The depot was damaged on 1 April 1916 when Zeppelin No. L11 bombed the town, killing 22 people and injuring 100 more.

TRAM CONDUCTRESSES in 1916 at the Wheatsheaf tram depot. The first ten conductresses were employed in June 1915 but eventually all of the conductors were women.

STAFF OF MONKWEARMOUTH STATION in the 1920s. On the wall '1000 mile tickets' are advertised. A broom of that size could probably do not only the platforms but also the roof!

STATION STAFF at the north end of the central station in around 1910.

BAR STAFF OF THE BLUEBELL PUBLIC HOUSE in around 1926. This was the public bar. As well as bottled Worthington the customers could feast on 'Packer's Celebrated Pies'.

THE BREWERY OF C. VAUX & SONS LTD. This is probably the Castle Street brewery somewhere between 1900 and 1914. At that time the firm employed 200 staff and owned about 150 licensed houses in the district. Then as now their horse-drawn drays were a feature of the town, 'Messrs Vaux's turn-outs being justly noted in the neighbourhood for smartness.' Very large numbers of horses were employed in towns for draught purposes and, given the fact that a horse deposits between four and six tons of manure a year, they added to the flavour of the environment in other ways.

ONE OF THE LORRIES OF VAUX LTD in the inter-war years. 'Highly Nourishing Stout' delivered at a speed of 12 m.p.h.!

CAPTAIN ERNEST VAUX and some of the men who served with him during the Boer War. The famous 'Double Maxim' owed its name and origin to the war. In tribute to the power of the maxim gun Vaux produced an extra strong beer which bore an image of the gun on its label. The young man standing on the extreme right is a William Stafford Sanderson who worked at Vaux Brewery then went on to run his own wine and spirits business on the quayside. Later he moved to Morpeth where he was mayor five times and where there is still a Sanderson Street.

TERRITORIAL SOLDIERS of the 7th Durham Light Infantry (Sunderland) at the Garrison Field.

WOMEN WORKERS AT A SOUP KITCHEN in the 1920s. This one was in High Street East. Soup kitchens were provided by a variety of bodies such as the parish councils, the churches and the police. They catered not only for the unemployed but also for children whose parents were out of work. In the latter case the children were given tickets by their teachers.

A HORSE AND CART OF THE NORTHERN LAUNDRY. The firm started in the 1880s and operated until the 1960s. Householders filled a 'bag wash' which was collected by horse and cart. The charge in the 1920s was 2s. 6d. per 'bag wash'.

WORKERS AT THE NORTHERN LAUNDRY. The firm had a depot in St Mark's Road. This photograph, and probably the horse and cart shown above may be from the pre-1914 period.

MAGGIE O'HARE in Moorgate Street in 1950. This lady, whose real name was Mrs Bulmer, was one of the last of the Sunderland fishwives. She used to sell crabs outside the old *Echo* office. (*Echo*)

A BILL STICKER in around 1892. It may be that the team referred to on the posters is the Sunderland Albion, which was formed in 1888 largely as a result of the efforts of James Allan who had fallen out with Sunderland AFC, which he had helped to establish. It played at the Blue House Field. The club went into liquidation in 1892.

MRS ELIZABETH RACKSTRAW, midwife. Mrs Rack-straw (1868–1942), Mrs Chambers and Mrs Fisher were the three certified midwives for Hendon. Mrs Rackstraw delivered 7,000 babies into the world including Billy Bell. Her finest hour came when she delivered the triplets of Mrs Achison of Hartley Street. She had seven children of her own. She lived in 32 Henry Street East where, in 1925, her daughter Henrietta was murdered by her boyfriend John Strong, who then committed suicide.

A FRENCH ONION MAN in the 1950s. Such men would usually come to Britain each year and spend two or three months in the country.

MEN WHO WORKED AT THE OLD MARKET in Coronation Street in the 1930s. Some of these worked on the roundabout which was a permanent feature. It was run in the 1930s by a Jimmy Stores who also ran a 'hit-the-goalie' stall. Also popular were the book and comic stall of Joe Arrowsmith (especially the huge collection of American comics), the large sweet stall (which did a roaring trade in cough candy) and the polished brass weighing machine which was used for the 'fattest person in Sunderland' competition. (*Echo*)

THE HOT POTATO MAN. Mr Rear was the verger at Holy Trinity. He used to stand at the corner of Bedford Street where he was able to supply the crowds of people leaving the Royal Cinema. (*Echo*)

THE STAFF OF GARDEN STREET SCHOOL in 1890. Many of the staff of the Board School – as in the voluntary schools – were unqualified assistants. In 1879 the Board only had 16 head teachers and 28 assistant teachers, and of the latter only 6 were certificated. By 1910 the total number of assistants was 532 and 300 of them were certificated.

WORKERS AT BRADMAN'S JAM FACTORY in Hendon Street in the 1920s.

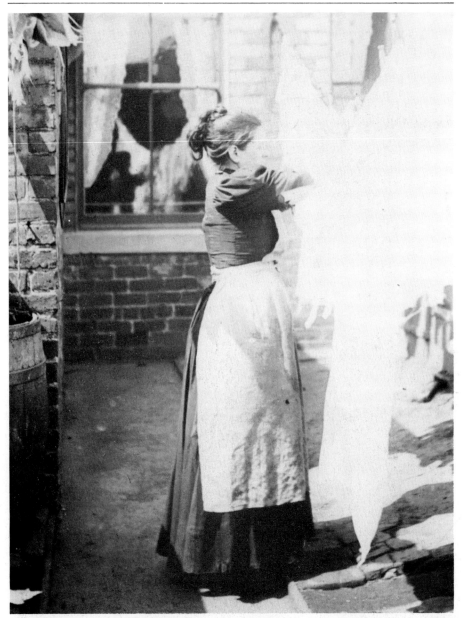

MISS ALLEN HANGING OUT HER WASHING in the backyard of her home in Paxton Terrace in 1897. Diamond Hall School is very near. The photograph was taken by her father. No doubt his daughter could have found better things for him to do with his time. There are very few photographs of this sort of routine domestic activity precisely because it was so mundane.

Some of the 'Bairns'

Sunderland may have known poverty, hard times and squalor, but respectable working class wives and mothers were as houseproud here as anywhere and no less determined that their children should be clean and well dressed when on show. Left to their own devices and in their natural backstreet environment, however, children can convey a very different impression, easily exaggerated by photographers keen to add support to moves for social reform. Of course, there were always destitute, ragged children who were without homes or caring families, and photographs of some of these are included in various social reports. The problem is in distinguishing the real 'street arabs' from the temporary ones!

A GROUP OF CHILDREN in around 1910. There is no indication as to the reason for this grouping. It is thought to be in the back lane of Addison Street or Robinson Street. There are also two dogs. It is a very effective photograph, whatever its purpose.

SUNDAY SCHOOL CHILDREN outside the Bethesda Mission in Hartley Street in 1900. The Mission was established in 1885. It was very popular with the East End children. Its lantern slides of missionaries were, apparently, a great attraction. In the 1920s and 1930s the procedure was that if a child attended in the weeks before Christmas tickets were given, and if enough of these were acquired admission was gained to the Christmas Magic Lantern Show.

MR J. CAMERON'S SCHOOL. The British and Foreign School Society moved their school from its site in Nicholson Street to a new one on the corner of Norfolk Street and Borough Road in 1856. It was next to the meeting house of the Quakers in Nile Street. At that time the headmaster of the school was the Scot Robert Cameron, who was still there when this photograph was taken in 1884.

THE BAND OF THE ORPHAN ASYLUM in 1900. The Orphan Asylum was designed in the Italianate manner by Childs and Lucas of London. It was opened in 1861. It held fifty boys. They were trained for seafaring careers. In the playground there was an old wreck called the *Victoria*. The building is now used by the East Community Centre.

MEMBERS OF THE OFFERTON SCOUT TROOP. The very first scout troop to be formed was Vaux's Own which is still in existence at the time of writing. Colonel Vaux was a friend of Robert Baden-Powell and shared his views.

GIRLS KNITTING IN A CLASSROOM. There is no evidence as to the date or school although somewhere around 1910 seems likely. There are forty-six girls. One of the framed pictures on the wall is, inevitably, Grace Darling rescuing the survivors of the wreck of the *Forfarshire*. The teacher seems to be fond of potted plants judging from the collection on the window sill, which is high enough to prevent distraction from outside.

CHILDREN DOING DRILL in the yard of an East End school. Again, there is no evidence as to either the date or the school. At first it seems to be girls alone but there are several boys. The value of learning the goose step seems rather questionable.

A MIXED CLASS in St Patrick's Roman Catholic School in around 1910. This school was established in the 1860s and was actually held in the church for almost a decade before transferring to Coronation Street. There are thirty-six children visible.

VALLEY ROAD SCHOOL CRICKET TEAM. Valley Road School was a Board School, opened in 1885 and holding 1,700 pupils. This photograph was taken in around 1928. The team had won the Schools' Cup for cricket. Mr Wilson the headmaster is on the right. On his right is Mr Watson. On the left is Mr Herdman who went on to become a headmaster in his own right. On his left is 'Buck' Jones.

CHILDREN OF HENDON INFANTS' SCHOOL in 1897. The group of children is shown with Miss Allison (in the hat) and Miss Bubb. The headmaster was also skipper of the lifeboat so the school was closed regularly whenever wrecks occurred. One ex-pupil remembered the boys having to knit scarfs on long wooden needles, which were then pulled out and restarted, again and again, to provide constant employment.

AN OUTING BY FULWELL SCHOOLCHILDREN in 1905. The venue is the corner of Sea Road opposite the Bluebell. Fulwell can only recently have been added to the electric tramways system so an outing on one of these vehicles would have been an adventure.

THE CORONATION PROCESSION of Fulwell schoolchildren in 1911. The view is down Sea Road.

ACKNOWLEDGEMENTS

Our thanks are due to the following for their assistance in the compilation and production of this book: Mr Stuart Bell of the *Echo* for permission to use photographs from its archives; Mr Frank Manders of Newcastle Central Library for permission to use photographs from the Auty-Hastings Collection; Mr Colin Meddes for permission to use photographs from the William Waples Collection; Messrs Philip Hall, Michael White, Neil Sinclair and their colleagues at the Sunderland Central Library and Museum for their friendship over the years and their help which is always forthcoming in unstinted measure; Mr Martin Preston who, while he might have a vested interest as a bookshop manager, is always very supportive of such ventures and was a prime mover in this one; Ms Paula Devlin for typing the text and captions with breathtaking speed and for quietly improving the careless punctuation; Mr Alan Owen for the details of the story about 'Double Maxim' and of the career of Mr Sanderson of Morpeth.

The thanks of Stuart Miller are also due to his co-editor, 'Billy' Bell BEM, from whose amazing collection the bulk of these photographs are taken and from whose memory much of the information in the captions is drawn. His great contribution to keeping alive the image of the Wearside of the past for the people of its present is invaluable. Nor must the long suffering support of his lovely wife Sally be forgotten!